EMMANUEL JOSEPH

Ephemeral Equilibrium, Navigating the Spheres of Wellness, Wealth, and Emotional Bonds

Copyright © 2025 by Emmanuel Joseph

All rights reserved. No part of this publication may be reproduced, stored or transmitted in any form or by any means, electronic, mechanical, photocopying, recording, scanning, or otherwise without written permission from the publisher. It is illegal to copy this book, post it to a website, or distribute it by any other means without permission.

First edition

*This book was professionally typeset on Reedsy.
Find out more at reedsy.com*

Contents

1	Chapter 1: The Balancing Act of Life	1
2	Chapter 2: The Foundations of Wellness	3
3	Chapter 3: The Pillars of Financial Health	5
4	Chapter 4: The Dynamics of Emotional Bonds	7
5	Chapter 5: The Interplay of Wellness and Wealth	9
6	Chapter 6: The Influence of Emotional Bonds on Wellness and...	11
7	Chapter 7: The Role of Self-Care in Ephemeral Equilibrium	13
8	Chapter 8: The Power of Mindfulness	15
9	Chapter 9: The Art of Letting Go	17
10	Chapter 10: The Practice of Gratitude	19
11	Chapter 11: The Power of Positive Thinking	21
12	Chapter 12: The Role of Resilience in Ephemeral Equilibrium	23
13	Chapter 13: The Importance of Setting Boundaries	25
14	Chapter 14: The Practice of Self-Compassion	27
15	Chapter 15: The Journey Towards Ephemeral Equilibrium	29

1

Chapter 1: The Balancing Act of Life

In the intricate dance of life, balance is not a static achievement but a dynamic pursuit. Wellness, wealth, and emotional bonds are the three spheres that often seem to orbit in a chaotic trajectory. One moment, you might find yourself enjoying a blissful state of health, only to be burdened by financial woes the next. Conversely, the thrill of financial success can sometimes come at the cost of strained relationships or neglected well-being. The challenge lies in recognizing that these spheres are not isolated but interconnected, each influencing the others in profound ways. The key to navigating this complex terrain lies in understanding and appreciating the fluid nature of balance.

The concept of ephemeral equilibrium suggests that balance is fleeting and subject to constant change. Unlike a tightrope walker who remains steady by maintaining a single focus, our lives require continuous adjustments and reevaluations. This dynamic approach calls for a mindset shift, where the pursuit of balance becomes a process of ongoing realignment rather than an end goal. Embracing the ephemeral nature of equilibrium allows us to be more adaptable and resilient, fostering a sense of harmony amidst life's inevitable fluctuations.

One effective strategy for achieving ephemeral equilibrium is to cultivate mindfulness and self-awareness. By being present in each moment and attuned to our inner and outer environments, we can make more informed decisions that support our overall well-being. This involves setting clear priorities, recognizing our limitations, and being willing to make adjustments as needed. It also requires a willingness to let go of the illusion of perfection and embrace the beauty of impermanence.

Ultimately, the journey towards ephemeral equilibrium is deeply personal and unique to each individual. It requires a commitment to self-reflection and a willingness to explore new perspectives and approaches. By embracing the fluid nature of balance and cultivating mindfulness, we can navigate the spheres of wellness, wealth, and emotional bonds with greater ease and grace.

2

Chapter 2: The Foundations of Wellness

Wellness is a multifaceted concept that encompasses physical, mental, and emotional health. At its core, wellness is about creating a state of balance and harmony within ourselves and our surroundings. This requires a holistic approach that addresses all aspects of our being, from the foods we eat and the activities we engage in, to the thoughts we think and the relationships we nurture.

Physical wellness is often the most tangible and immediate aspect of our overall well-being. It involves maintaining a healthy body through regular exercise, proper nutrition, and adequate rest. Physical wellness also includes preventive measures such as regular check-ups, vaccinations, and self-care practices that support our body's natural healing processes. By prioritizing physical wellness, we create a strong foundation for overall health and vitality.

Mental wellness is equally important and involves cultivating a positive mindset, managing stress, and nurturing our intellectual growth. This can be achieved through practices such as meditation, mindfulness, and engaging in activities that challenge and stimulate our minds. Mental wellness also requires addressing any underlying psychological issues and seeking professional support when needed. By nurturing our mental well-being, we enhance our capacity for resilience and emotional stability.

Emotional wellness involves being in tune with our feelings and emotions, and developing healthy ways to express and manage them. This includes building strong emotional intelligence, fostering supportive relationships, and practicing self-compassion. Emotional wellness also involves recognizing and addressing any unresolved emotional issues or traumas that may be affecting our overall well-being. By prioritizing emotional wellness, we create a sense of inner peace and fulfillment that supports our overall health and happiness.

3

Chapter 3: The Pillars of Financial Health

Financial health is a critical component of our overall well-being, influencing our ability to meet our basic needs, achieve our goals, and enjoy a sense of security and stability. Achieving financial health requires a combination of practical strategies, informed decision-making, and a healthy mindset towards money.

The first pillar of financial health is financial literacy. This involves understanding basic financial concepts such as budgeting, saving, investing, and managing debt. Financial literacy empowers us to make informed decisions about our money and build a solid foundation for long-term financial success. It also involves being aware of our financial habits and patterns, and making adjustments as needed to support our financial goals.

The second pillar is financial planning. This involves setting clear financial goals, creating a budget, and developing a plan to achieve those goals. Financial planning also includes setting aside funds for emergencies, retirement, and other long-term needs. By having a clear financial plan in place, we can navigate the uncertainties of life with greater confidence and ease.

The third pillar is financial resilience. This involves building a strong financial foundation that can withstand unexpected challenges and setbacks. Financial resilience includes having adequate savings, diversifying our income streams, and protecting ourselves with insurance and other risk management strategies. By building financial resilience, we can weather the storms of life and maintain our financial health in the face of adversity.

Finally, the fourth pillar is financial wellness. This involves cultivating a healthy relationship with money and aligning our financial decisions with our values and priorities. Financial wellness includes being mindful of our spending habits, practicing gratitude and contentment, and giving back to our communities. By prioritizing financial wellness, we create a sense of abundance and fulfillment that supports our overall well-being.

4

Chapter 4: The Dynamics of Emotional Bonds

Emotional bonds are the invisible threads that connect us to others and play a crucial role in our overall well-being. These bonds are formed through shared experiences, mutual support, and genuine care and affection. The quality of our emotional bonds can significantly impact our mental and emotional health, influencing our sense of belonging, self-worth, and happiness.

One of the most important aspects of emotional bonds is effective communication. Clear, honest, and empathetic communication helps build trust and understanding in our relationships. It involves not only expressing our thoughts and feelings but also actively listening and being present for others. By fostering open and respectful communication, we create a strong foundation for healthy and meaningful connections.

Another key factor in nurturing emotional bonds is mutual support. This involves being there for each other in times of need, offering encouragement, and celebrating each other's successes. Mutual support also includes being willing to give and receive help, and recognizing the importance of interdependence in our relationships. By cultivating a culture of mutual support, we strengthen our emotional bonds and create a sense of community and belonging.

Emotional bonds also require a deep sense of empathy and compassion. This involves putting ourselves in others' shoes and understanding their perspectives and feelings. Empathy helps us connect on a deeper level and fosters a sense of closeness and intimacy in our relationships. Compassion, on the other hand, involves showing kindness and understanding towards ourselves and others, especially during challenging times. By practicing empathy and compassion, we create a nurturing environment that supports the growth and well-being of our emotional bonds.

Finally, emotional bonds thrive on shared experiences and meaningful interactions. This involves spending quality time together, creating memories, and engaging in activities that bring joy and fulfillment. Shared experiences help build a sense of connection and create lasting bonds that withstand the test of time. By prioritizing meaningful interactions, we invest in the health and longevity of our emotional bonds.

5

Chapter 5: The Interplay of Wellness and Wealth

The spheres of wellness and wealth are deeply interconnected, each influencing the other in profound ways. Our physical, mental, and emotional well-being can significantly impact our financial health, and vice versa. Understanding this interplay is crucial for achieving a balanced and fulfilling life.

Physical wellness, for example, is essential for maintaining our ability to work and earn a living. Poor health can lead to medical expenses, reduced productivity, and even loss of income. On the other hand, financial stress can take a toll on our physical health, leading to issues such as hypertension, insomnia, and weakened immune function. By prioritizing physical wellness, we can enhance our financial health and create a more stable and secure future.

Mental wellness also plays a critical role in our financial health. A positive mindset and emotional stability can enhance our ability to make sound financial decisions, manage stress, and stay focused on our goals. Conversely, financial problems can contribute to anxiety, depression, and other mental health issues. By nurturing our mental wellness, we can improve our financial resilience and create a sense of abundance and fulfillment.

Emotional wellness is equally important in the realm of wealth. Strong emotional bonds and supportive relationships can provide a sense of security and stability that enhances our financial well-being. Conversely, financial stress can strain our relationships and create emotional turmoil. By prioritizing emotional wellness, we can strengthen our support networks and create a more harmonious and prosperous life.

Ultimately, the interplay of wellness and wealth is a dynamic and ongoing process. It requires a holistic approach that addresses all aspects of our being and recognizes the interconnectedness of our physical, mental, and emotional health. By nurturing our wellness and wealth in tandem, we can create a more balanced and fulfilling life.

6

Chapter 6: The Influence of Emotional Bonds on Wellness and Wealth

Emotional bonds play a crucial role in our overall well-being and financial health. Our relationships with family, friends, and loved ones can provide a sense of support, security, and fulfillment that enhances our physical, mental, and emotional health. Conversely, strained relationships and emotional turmoil can take a toll on our well-being and financial health.

One of the most significant ways emotional bonds influence our wellness is through social support. Strong emotional bonds provide a network of support that can help us navigate life's challenges and stressors. This support can take many forms, including emotional encouragement, practical assistance, and even financial help. By nurturing our emotional bonds, we create a safety net that enhances our resilience and overall well-being.

Emotional bonds also play a critical role in our mental health. Positive relationships can boost our mood, enhance our self-esteem, and provide a sense of purpose and belonging. Conversely, toxic relationships and emotional conflict can contribute to anxiety, depression, and other mental health issues. By prioritizing healthy and supportive relationships, we can improve our mental wellness and create a more positive sense of well-being.

Emotional bonds also have a significant impact on our financial health.

Positive relationships can provide a sense of security and stability that enhances our ability to make sound financial decisions and pursue our goals. Conversely, strained relationships and emotional conflict can lead to financial stress and instability. By nurturing our emotional bonds, we create a support system that enhances our financial resilience and overall well-being.

Ultimately, the influence of emotional bonds on wellness and wealth is profound and far-reaching. By prioritizing our relationships and cultivating a culture of mutual support, empathy, and compassion, we can enhance our overall well-being and create a more balanced and fulfilling life.

7

Chapter 7: The Role of Self-Care in Ephemeral Equilibrium

Self-care is a fundamental practice that supports our overall well-being and helps us maintain ephemeral equilibrium. It involves taking deliberate actions to care for our physical, mental, and emotional health, and recognizing the importance of self-compassion and self-awareness.

Physical self-care includes practices such as regular exercise, proper nutrition, and adequate rest. It also involves taking preventive measures such as regular check-ups, vaccinations, and self-care practices that support our body's natural healing processes. By prioritizing physical self-care, we create a strong foundation for overall health and vitality.

Mental self-care involves cultivating a positive mindset, managing stress, and nurturing our intellectual growth. This can be achieved through practices such as meditation, mindfulness, and engaging in activities that challenge and stimulate our minds. Mental self-care also requires addressing any underlying psychological issues and seeking professional support when needed. By nurturing our mental well-being, we enhance our capacity for resilience and emotional stability.

Emotional self-care involves being in tune with our feelings and emotions, and developing healthy ways to express and manage them. This includes building strong emotional intelligence, fostering supportive relationships, and practicing self-compassion. Emotional self-care also involves recognizing and addressing any unresolved emotional issues or traumas that may be affecting our overall well-being. By prioritizing emotional self-care, we create a sense of inner peace and fulfillment that supports our overall health and happiness.

Ultimately, self-care is a personal and unique practice that requires ongoing commitment and self-awareness. By prioritizing self-care and making it an integral part of our daily lives, we can enhance our overall well-being and maintain ephemeral equilibrium in the face of life's challenges and fluctuations.

8

Chapter 8: The Power of Mindfulness

Mindfulness is a powerful practice that can help us navigate the spheres of wellness, wealth, and emotional bonds with greater ease and grace. It involves being present in each moment, fully aware of our thoughts, feelings, and surroundings, and accepting them without judgment.

Mindfulness supports our overall well-being by helping us cultivate a sense of inner peace and clarity. It can enhance our physical health by reducing stress and promoting relaxation. Regular mindfulness practice has been shown to lower blood pressure, improve sleep quality, and boost immune function. By prioritizing mindfulness, we create a strong foundation for physical wellness.

Mindfulness also supports our mental well-being by helping us manage stress, anxiety, and negative emotions. It involves being aware of our thoughts and feelings and accepting them without judgment. This practice can enhance our emotional stability and resilience, allowing us to navigate life's challenges with greater ease. By prioritizing mindfulness, we create a sense of mental clarity and emotional balance.

Mindfulness can also enhance our financial well-being by helping us make more informed and intentional financial decisions. It involves being aware of our financial habits and patterns and making adjustments as needed to support our financial goals. Mindfulness can also help us cultivate a healthy relationship with money and align our financial decisions with our values and priorities. By prioritizing mindfulness, we create a sense of financial clarity and abundance.

Finally, mindfulness can enhance our emotional bonds by helping us be more present and attentive in our relationships. It involves being fully aware of our interactions with others and responding with empathy and compassion. Mindfulness can also help us manage conflict and build stronger, more meaningful connections. By prioritizing mindfulness, we create a sense of emotional clarity and fulfillment that supports our overall well-being.

9

Chapter 9: The Art of Letting Go

Letting go is an essential practice for maintaining ephemeral equilibrium and navigating the spheres of wellness, wealth, and emotional bonds. It involves releasing attachments to outcomes, expectations, and past experiences that no longer serve our well-being.

In the realm of wellness, letting go can involve releasing unhealthy habits, patterns, and beliefs that undermine our physical, mental, and emotional health. This might include letting go of stress-inducing behaviors, negative self-talk, and unrealistic standards of perfection. By practicing letting go, we create space for healthier habits and more positive self-perceptions to take root.

In the realm of wealth, letting go can involve releasing financial stress and anxiety that stems from fear and scarcity. This might include letting go of rigid financial goals, unrealistic expectations, and limiting beliefs about money. By practicing letting go, we create space for financial abundance and a healthier relationship with wealth.

In the realm of emotional bonds, letting go can involve releasing attachments to relationships, expectations, and past hurts that no longer serve our well-being. This might include letting go of toxic relationships, unmet expectations, and unresolved emotional baggage. By practicing letting go, we create space for healthier relationships and more meaningful connections to flourish.

Ultimately, the art of letting go is about creating space for growth, healing, and transformation. It requires a willingness to release what no longer serves us and embrace the present moment with an open heart and mind. By practicing letting go, we can maintain ephemeral equilibrium and navigate the spheres of wellness, wealth, and emotional bonds with greater ease and grace.

10

Chapter 10: The Practice of Gratitude

Gratitude is a powerful practice that can enhance our overall well-being and help us maintain ephemeral equilibrium. It involves recognizing and appreciating the positive aspects of our lives, no matter how small or insignificant they may seem.

Practicing gratitude supports our physical wellness by promoting a positive mindset and reducing stress. Regular gratitude practice has been shown to lower blood pressure, improve sleep quality, and boost immune function. By prioritizing gratitude, we create a strong foundation for physical wellness.

Gratitude also supports our mental well-being by enhancing our emotional resilience and overall happiness. It involves focusing on the positive aspects of our lives and cultivating a sense of appreciation and contentment. Gratitude can also help us manage negative emotions and reduce feelings of anxiety and depression. By prioritizing gratitude, we create a sense of mental clarity and emotional balance.

Gratitude can also enhance our financial well-being by shifting our focus from scarcity to abundance. It involves recognizing and appreciating the financial resources and opportunities we have, no matter how small. Gratitude can also help us make more intentional and mindful financial decisions. By prioritizing gratitude, we create a sense of financial clarity and abundance.

Finally, gratitude can enhance our emotional bonds by fostering a sense of appreciation and connection in our relationships. It involves recognizing and appreciating the positive qualities and contributions of others. Gratitude can also help us build stronger, more meaningful connections and manage conflict with empathy and compassion. By prioritizing gratitude, we create a sense of emotional clarity and fulfillment that supports our overall well-being.

11

Chapter 11: The Power of Positive Thinking

Positive thinking is a powerful practice that can enhance our overall well-being and help us maintain ephemeral equilibrium. It involves cultivating a positive mindset and focusing on the positive aspects of our lives, even in the face of challenges and setbacks.

Positive thinking supports our physical wellness by reducing stress and promoting a sense of well-being. Regular positive thinking practice has been shown to lower blood pressure, improve sleep quality, and boost immune function. By prioritizing positive thinking, we create a strong foundation for physical wellness.

Positive thinking also supports our mental well-being by enhancing our emotional resilience and overall happiness. It involves focusing on the positive aspects of our lives and cultivating a sense of optimism and hope. Positive thinking can also help us manage negative emotions and reduce feelings of anxiety and depression. By prioritizing positive thinking, we create a sense of mental clarity and emotional balance.

Positive thinking can also enhance our financial well-being by shifting our focus from scarcity to abundance. It involves recognizing and appreciating the financial resources and opportunities we have, no matter how small. Positive thinking can also help us make more intentional and mindful financial decisions. By prioritizing positive thinking, we create a sense of financial clarity and abundance.

Finally, positive thinking can enhance our emotional bonds by fostering a sense of appreciation and connection in our relationships. It involves recognizing and appreciating the positive qualities and contributions of others. Positive thinking can also help us build stronger, more meaningful connections and manage conflict with empathy and compassion. By prioritizing positive thinking, we create a sense of emotional clarity and fulfillment that supports our overall well-being.

12

Chapter 12: The Role of Resilience in Ephemeral Equilibrium

Resilience is a critical quality that supports our overall well-being and helps us maintain ephemeral equilibrium. It involves the ability to adapt and bounce back from challenges, setbacks, and adversity.

Resilience supports our physical wellness by helping us cope with stress and recover from illness or injury. It involves maintaining a positive mindset, seeking support when needed, and practicing self-care. By prioritizing resilience, we create a strong foundation for physical wellness.

Resilience also supports our mental well-being by enhancing our emotional stability and overall happiness. It involves developing coping strategies, seeking support when needed, and maintaining a positive outlook. Resilience can also help us manage negative emotions and reduce feelings of anxiety and depression. By prioritizing resilience, we create a sense of mental clarity and emotional balance.

Resilience can also enhance our financial well-being by helping us navigate financial challenges and setbacks. It involves developing a strong financial foundation, seeking support when needed, and maintaining a positive outlook. Resilience can also help us make more informed and intentional financial decisions. By prioritizing resilience, we create a sense of financial clarity and abundance.

Finally, resilience can enhance our emotional bonds by helping us navigate relationship challenges and conflicts. It involves maintaining a positive outlook, seeking support when needed, patience and empathy. Resilience can also help us build stronger, more meaningful connections and manage conflict effectively. By prioritizing resilience, we create a sense of emotional clarity and fulfillment that supports our overall well-being.

13

Chapter 13: The Importance of Setting Boundaries

Setting boundaries is a crucial practice for maintaining ephemeral equilibrium and navigating the spheres of wellness, wealth, and emotional bonds. It involves establishing clear limits and expectations in our relationships, work, and personal lives to protect our well-being and create a sense of balance.

In the realm of wellness, setting boundaries can involve prioritizing self-care and saying no to activities or commitments that undermine our physical, mental, and emotional health. This might include setting limits on work hours, social engagements, and screen time. By setting boundaries, we create space for rest, relaxation, and activities that support our well-being.

In the realm of wealth, setting boundaries can involve managing our finances responsibly and making intentional financial decisions. This might include setting limits on spending, saving for future goals, and avoiding debt. By setting financial boundaries, we create a sense of financial stability and security.

In the realm of emotional bonds, setting boundaries can involve establishing clear limits and expectations in our relationships. This might include setting limits on emotional labor, maintaining healthy communication, and addressing any behaviors that undermine our well-being. By setting boundaries, we create a sense of respect and mutual understanding in our relationships.

Ultimately, setting boundaries is about protecting our well-being and creating a sense of balance in our lives. It requires a willingness to prioritize our needs and communicate our limits clearly and respectfully. By setting boundaries, we can maintain ephemeral equilibrium and navigate the spheres of wellness, wealth, and emotional bonds with greater ease and grace.

14

Chapter 14: The Practice of Self-Compassion

Self-compassion is a fundamental practice that supports our overall well-being and helps us maintain ephemeral equilibrium. It involves treating ourselves with kindness, understanding, and acceptance, especially in times of difficulty and self-doubt.

Self-compassion supports our physical wellness by promoting a sense of well-being and reducing stress. It involves recognizing our limitations and taking care of our bodies with kindness and respect. By prioritizing self-compassion, we create a strong foundation for physical wellness.

Self-compassion also supports our mental well-being by enhancing our emotional resilience and overall happiness. It involves treating ourselves with kindness and understanding, especially in times of failure and self-doubt. Self-compassion can also help us manage negative emotions and reduce feelings of anxiety and depression. By prioritizing self-compassion, we create a sense of mental clarity and emotional balance.

Self-compassion can also enhance our financial well-being by helping us cultivate a healthy relationship with money and make more intentional financial decisions. It involves treating ourselves with kindness and understanding, especially in times of financial stress and uncertainty. Self-compassion can also help us shift our focus from scarcity to abundance and create a sense of financial clarity and fulfillment.

Finally, self-compassion can enhance our emotional bonds by fostering a sense of empathy and connection in our relationships. It involves treating ourselves with kindness and understanding, which in turn allows us to treat others with empathy and compassion. Self-compassion can also help us manage conflict and build stronger, more meaningful connections. By prioritizing self-compassion, we create a sense of emotional clarity and fulfillment that supports our overall well-being.

15

Chapter 15: The Journey Towards Ephemeral Equilibrium

The journey towards ephemeral equilibrium is a dynamic and ongoing process that requires continuous self-reflection, adaptation, and growth. It involves recognizing the interconnectedness of the spheres of wellness, wealth, and emotional bonds, and embracing the fluid nature of balance.

Throughout this journey, it is important to cultivate mindfulness and self-awareness, practice self-care and self-compassion, and set clear boundaries to protect our well-being. It also requires a willingness to let go of attachments and expectations that no longer serve us, and to embrace the present moment with an open heart and mind.

The journey towards ephemeral equilibrium is deeply personal and unique to each individual. It requires a commitment to exploring new perspectives and approaches, and to making continuous adjustments and realignments. By embracing the dynamic nature of balance and prioritizing our overall well-being, we can navigate the spheres of wellness, wealth, and emotional bonds with greater ease and grace.

Ultimately, the journey towards ephemeral equilibrium is about creating a life that is rich in meaning, purpose, and fulfillment. It involves recognizing and appreciating the beauty of impermanence, and embracing the ebb and flow of life's challenges and opportunities. By prioritizing our overall well-being and nurturing our relationships, we can create a sense of harmony and balance that supports our overall health and happiness.

Book description: Ephemeral Equilibrium: Navigating the Spheres of Wellness, Wealth, and Emotional Bonds

In the chaotic dance of life, finding balance is a constant pursuit, not a fixed state. *Ephemeral Equilibrium* explores the delicate interplay between wellness, wealth, and emotional bonds, offering a dynamic approach to achieving harmony in these interconnected spheres. This book delves into the essence of wellness, financial health, and the power of relationships, emphasizing the fluid nature of balance and the importance of adaptability.

Through fifteen insightful chapters, readers will embark on a journey of self-discovery and growth, learning how to cultivate mindfulness, set boundaries, and practice self-compassion. Each chapter offers practical strategies and profound reflections, encouraging readers to embrace the transient nature of equilibrium and find fulfillment amidst life's inevitable fluctuations.

Whether you seek to enhance your physical and mental well-being, achieve financial resilience, or nurture meaningful connections, *Ephemeral Equilibrium* provides the guidance and inspiration needed to navigate the complexities of modern life with grace and wisdom. This book is a must-read for anyone striving to create a life rich in meaning, purpose, and joy.

www.ingramcontent.com/pod-product-compliance
Lightning Source LLC
LaVergne TN
LVHW021055100526
838202LV00083B/6098